POEMS
FOR
THE
ASYLUM

POEMS
FOR
THE
ASYLUM

DANIEL J. LUTZ

atmosphere press

Introduction

These poems were written over several months while I was in and out of various mental health facilities while being treated for my various illnesses and emotional breakdowns of perhaps some of the toughest moments of my life.

They study the human condition in repeating themes that are viewed from many angles to compose a complete picture of the complicated existence we all struggle with. The simple language searches for poetic conciseness, lending the concepts a deeper power as they strive to record my feelings, thoughts, experiences and often desperate strivings.

Table of Contents

Last Yesterday

Our conversation of last night
tilted me back towards despair.
I'm glad for that.
I was feeling too happy,
too rushed,
it was all too easy.
I was worried I wouldn't
work too hard.

A brave heart beats solemnly,
slowly.
It expands for truth, integrity,
justice, honor,
love.
I lack all but the last.

I'm clinging to you
like a tree grown
on a cliff edge,
snaking tangled roots into you carefully,
watching you for erosion,
for your wild weather
and gentle storms.

Beyond reason,
past hope,
farther than faith,
I'm asking for you
to grasp me back.

Blue Painting

I couldn't keep her
from drowning.
I watched her sink away
into the cold green.
I let go
as she desperately
grabbed air, expecting
my hand.
I watched her fall in slow motion
beneath the barely rippling water.
She fell forever,
through bottomless depths.
She's still,
arms out-stretched,
scared eyes pleading to me.
I just stared at her
from my dead world
above the waves.

Solitude

Life is the hinge
of dusty moth wings,
a piano in the rain,
rubble,
wind chimes on the porch
in the morning,
the skeletons of trees,
birds pressed against the sky
and an empty room
with only me in it.

Leviathan

My nature is such
that only sailors
and drowning men
can see me
Swift
Secretive
Soundless
A deep starving shadow
Abyss

Walking Ahead

There's a broken butterfly,
crashed and crumpled
in the still wet sand
where the tide has receded.
Webbed seagull prints
and bits of shells are strewn
where it lays,
while ants crawl on
the bent and faded wings.

Out past the rift
in the brown and gray clouds,
the rounded horizon shows
where the Earth curves.
Crouched over the crumbling
insect, studying it,
hearing the waves talk
to the pebbles and the beach.
I'm ruminating on how far you feel,
though it is actually
me who is away

Tumult

She can't carry us
not all of us
I can't carry myself
let alone carry her
while she carries everyone else
and me
So I let her alone
and then she was gone
and then she wasn't there
and then I was alone
unable to carry anything
or anyone
especially me
and not her,
never her
and then I wasn't there
gone

then she wasn't there
and then she was gone

The Tormented

Wrap your sky around me
press against me your tender bones
your warm cloud
forgive me your torment
your tormentor your beast
cloaked in love and splendor
sorrow
comfort me your sacrifice
and love me still
make me quiet
share me all that I slashed
and gnarled
undeservedly I beg you forgive me
my trespasses
help me resist fear
solve the calculus of my problem
provide me your patience
I want to glow you again
heat your home too precious to live in

Bastion

Do not think that
I have not been to
the very bottom of
my own depths.
Light was the supposed
beginning,
but there was long dark time
before
and I am obsessed with it:
the insidious, lurking quiet;
the calm place
to become obscured
in the embrace of sadness;
to disappear into its distance;
to be unafraid;
to cease.

Danger is the day:
risky, real, raw exposure
where vulnerabilities are visible,
brazen, bare, bold and elephant.
Without cover,
without cower,
I hide behind eyes without pain.

I am not all black.
I am not white.
There is no gray,
except the gravel and the rain.
There is opacity
and there is oblivion.

There Goes Hope

I have to stay with the feelings:
the loss,
the hurt, fear, sorrow,
regret.
Avoiding them, denying them,
dishonors the reality.
I created the truths that I have destroyed,
the pain I have left in others
because I loved them, because
I broke them, because
they are broken
and I am left.
Hope is fleeting.

The Constantly Changing Confusion is Continuously Continuous and Confusing

There are never any faces
in my dreams,
only parts of people,
places and objects,
the rest filled in with understanding
and knowledge of what is there
without being seen.
The blackness of black
is not all black,
there is white in the dark,
ravens in the wood
and distortions in the carefully blurred
lines, a combination of scribble
and concise.
Something is always watching.
Fear is absolutely absolute.

Reading Haikus

Safe and shorn
Stern and determined
Sure
Solid
and certain
Sacrificing and
same
Consistent and surfaced
Serious
Centered
Solace and
Solitude
Sanctuary

the sun sinks into a world of trees
whose leaves pain the clouds.
What are you dreaming of
when you move your wings?

Amalgamate

a flock of little brown birds flits
to the ground
like falling leaves.
parts and pieces
of varied thoughts
and difficult feelings
amalgamate with fragments
of complex feelings
and difficult thoughts
shaping one emotion without a name.
I'm fumbling with the white
and the absence of rain.
my grip on hope slips.

Loss

The night is a passing thing
only for most
Sorrow is a bird
with a broken wing
I'm sorry I made you
afraid to love me
It's painful to sleep
and it hurts to be alive
Everything is worse without you

Unsafety

You're so meek, weak, small and far
when you tell me you love me
It gives me such sorrow
to know how I have made you
so afraid, so hurt, so full of pain
and broken you so deeply,
so completely
that you are unsafe to love me.
I am unsafe to love,
to be loved,
to be your beloved
and your lover.
Despite all my efforts,
I keep marking your wall
and so, I prepare
to leave myself.

Pilfer and Plunder/Spoils and Smattering/Covert/Grown

I've lived my life throwing shadows
colluding with my eyes
to see what's not there
another fright from out of darkness
I've lived my lies smattering pain
covering my tries without shame
hiding eyes woven from the darkness
another flight into the pain
I lied about my life creating shadows
adding more darkness to the shame
some kind of night woven out of blame
trying to be what's not there
another darkness sewn out of shadows
the pain grown out of lies and shame
some kind of loneliness made out of pain
I've lived my life enclosed in shadows

Jumbles

It's convoluted
my thoughts,
my mind, my feelings,
time,
the way I move
through these things,
the way I treat you,
love you, care for you,
don't care for you,
my wandering through anger,
hurt, sadness, and drowning.
Hope is pain is hopelessness.
They are convoluted,
my memories, beliefs,
my myths and legends,
the stories I tell myself about
my life, my dreams and loses,
perceptions and other
miscellaneous abstractions,
my fears meshed with misery,
agony, despair, my multifacetedness.
Today is the first day I wanted
To go outside.
Momentum.
Evacuation.
Wind in the leaves turning colors.
I see what I'm saying.

Intrusion

a general of one,
fighting an invisible enemy,
entire armies of emotions,
using metaphorical tactics
and metaphysical blades.

it is the heart of the warrior
that encapsulating force
and driving will
that compels them to march
into the ranks
of their opponents.

I can see the world outside,
but I need to feel it
if I am to survive.
it is the war within though,
that must be won.

Note in a Notebook

Little lies
become big lies become
hurt, pain, shame
and tumble.
We cannot force
our lives to be the dishonesty we
tell others about ourselves.
We can however,
shape our being
with truth
and considered actions.

Serendipity, Mosaic

She gives to me
of her heart
to replace the pieces
mine is missing.
She holds me,
lets me lean inside
her warm depths
when mine are swarming:
flaws, flaws, lack of symmetry,
disconnection
and flaws.

Back and forth, broken mind, inside out–
emotions aren't the problem.
The problem is thinking
emotions are the problem.
When you describe the chair,
it ceases to be a chair
and just becomes a thing.

I have become just a thing:
a dim light in a silent forest,
with unseen forces combining and
killing each other to live,
even if only for a minute more.
Serendipity.
The parts of me that I used
to believe in, weren't even real,
just a sad mosaic
of an imagined hero.

The Fall

I have saved these pictures of you,
for your song.
I try to save your love.
I really want to be there with you,
with the clouds behind you.

I didn't want to change.
I wasn't looking back,
wasn't trying.
I just let sleep erase our dreams,
my dream of you.

A human multitude
of pain and shame,
of frayed and ragged love.
I didn't understand my hidden worlds
were hurting you.

My heart was beating right,
my head was not.
A thief, a bandit of your soul,
I was not there to catch you
if you fell.

Ideations

I daydream of dying,
laying down and
not getting up,
releasing the pain; the sorrow; the hurt;
regret; shame; self-loathing; fear;
the wooden, lonely, empty, hopelessness;
the agonizing, overwhelming, intense misery;
the turmoil; the debilitating, crippling,
disabling depths of depression
that reduces me to
survival second by second.

I daydream of death,
escape, a fantasy of endless sleep,
a comforting unreality,
peace, salvation, oblivion,
quiet slumber forever.
What keeps me here is not love,
concern, wanting, striving, interest, hope,
belief, faith, beauty, trust, passion, caring,
but my inability to override the innate
will to live.
So only I daydream
My deadly wish.

Hallway

When he passed me the note
that had "Friend" written shakily
on the outside,
winter had already awoken
in the cold,
dark
arctic of my soul.
He said nothing.
I hesitated,
took a long breath
and paused
before I undid the many folds.

Each letter had uncarefully been
gone over many times in black.
It read only,
"Pride is
a dim
lamp on a
Dark
Road".
I let out my breath,
Felt my hopelessness.

After staring at it
for many moments,
I wonder now
if he sees the glow
from far off in the solemn night
illuminating his way
or if like me,
has he also resigned to give up?
The light doesn't let you see.

The Outside from Within

sputtering
muttering
sullen in slightest rain
little rivulets channel into cracked concrete
wind picks fading leaves
off lightly bending branches
gray lonely fog clings low
worms slug along muddy sidewalks
consumption of summer
tired sun behind indistinct sky
I wonder what it is like
to actually want to be alive

Insurrection

Which came first,
the wolf or the flower?
Beauty and decay:
ancient and magical forces
that mark the rapidly shifting
movements between man and mayhem.

I question,
wonder,
if I can subdue
all the terror and infinity
that has turned my body
into corruption.

One might as well ask
the land and the seas to give up
their hidden dead:
shallow shoals,
deepest graves
and empty cemeteries.

There is nothing left
to rise up except
the monster in me –
fangs and fur,
fatality and fury.

Ultimately, it matters not
which came first.
The wolf thrives on blood,
murder and carnage.
the flower lives
only to be beautiful, wilt and then to wither.

Desolations

All I think about is you
and dying.
There is starting not to be
a difference in those thoughts.
You are as much a fantasy
as my destruction,
only warmer and more lovely,
less final and complete.

I miss when your eyes
tell me you love me,
now only darker brown.
I'm fading from you,
drifting towards the sleep
without dreams.
The silent empty.

With my night wish,
I've slipped beyond understanding
of value and matter.
Nothing has a name
and it is mine.
I'm losing my time to take.

Journal Entry

I dwell in the cave
beyond the light,
in the black,
the dark, the damp
and the cold.
  Nothing comes in
which I do not bring.
Nothing means nothing is nothing.
  I live in the black, the nothingness.
I am the black,
the cold, the dark,
the loss of light,
the nothing.

Brazier/Pyre

It's deceiving in here
where the morning always is,
black and I'm bleeding
in places no one knows about.

Trying to understand
the light, I live on fire:
full of love and death;
a smoldering Fury;

tormented; tormenting;
a King; a killer;
a misfit; a misanthrope;
a dark, teeming hulk;

a bulky silhouette
against a shadow,
occasionally illuminated
by the undefined

shape am I:
inexorable,
lamenting,
melancholic,

insipient,
wistful for my
irrecoverable past.
Dead.

A Dirge

I don't want to play.
I don't feel like playing right now.
I don't want to return
to the land of Giants and Queens,
fading stars and scattered dreams.
Life is brutish, harsh, dastardly,
treacherous.
There is no plan,
no hidden splendor,
just continued drudgery
and filth.
There is no magic beanstalk
to treasure in the clouds,
no descent to fiery stones,
just banal pain,
agony,
defeat after defeat.
There is endless trudging
through stained misery
and octagons of sad, sad
sadness.
There are no buttercups
or rainbows in sweet mist
and glorious sunshine.
There isn't even glorious sunshine.
There is bullshit
and inevitable storms
and thunder

and spark crashing lightning
and dark, dark, black, darkness
and night without ends
and.
Once the enormous, clawed hand
of suffering suffocates you
within its constriction clutch,
it's powerful fear and
savage strength,
there is no more breath
in belief,
no hope,
no beauty.
There is just longing
to quit
and be proud
to do so,
to have the chance
to rest
by side
with nothingness.

Anxiety/Mania(c)

swarming
vibrating
painful squirming electric torso
shaky hands
feet have to move
knee bounce
falling and falling
and falling forever
and never knowing
if and when you'll smash
at the bottom of the pit
not knowing if there even is
a bottom
endless hopeless agony
misery
painful physical emotional rendering
of phantasmic fantastic existential angst
and doom impending
from without any source
without a reason
a place
trace
an ache
and insatiable ache
above your stomach
below your chest
filling your chest
your torso

vibrating squirming electric pain
until you feel that
one
more
second
is too much more
and then you have to endure
and endure
and endure
more falling crawling squirming
until you wish you
could
die
just to make it stop
anything to make it stop
even just for one minute
Stop
Fucking Stop
Please
and still
endure
endure
survive
is all you can really do

Reality Reassembled (in the Dominion of Dreams)/ (In love with Dying)

Life is a ghost
that haunts me
in my sleep.
I'd like to know instead
what it feels like
to hold you in a dream,
to disseminate the
undulating vacillations that
illuminate my illusions into you.
Let me creep into your spine.

Twist with me.
Brook with me.
Show me which space to love.
Hike me your softness.
Grow me in fields.
Bury me in flowers.
Rain on my face.

Wipe me of my soot.
Write me with words
unpoetic and cringing,
measure me with meter.
Make me patient
where I lack,
where I slide.
Keep me inside you
until the specter floats me
from the history
of my nightmares.

Homunculus/Unmanned

I keep forgetting my body;
the piles of eyes inside my skull;
the unholy immersion in
my heart full of rain;
the sorrow I breathe;
the insensate limbs which
marry me to the world outside;
the hollow helpless,
safe, comfortable, dangerous,
cautiously, fatally optimistic failings
of my being.

They keep remembering me though,
recreating reconnection to what has gone,
disassembling, disconnecting me
from what might be,
breaking the piece
of art I am,
could be, won't be,
was, wasn't,
will not be, were, would be,
am not, shant be.

Torn,
I am torn from me.
I keep forgetting that.

Disarray

the occasional drops
pock and dimple
only the puddles,
but are otherwise unseen.
The black cement,
morning gloom,
the loss in the trees,
silence,
dust on the gravel,
all paints a bleak picture of pain.
flickering streetlights dimly whisper
to one another of sadness
and dismay,
disarray.
I need to get more used
to being alone.

The Road Within

Twisting, winding, wandering, meandering
by brackish swamps and bleak,
dark, empty woodlands,
muddy streams and strands
of the road I am, paced
by sandy potholes
and gravely, grave turns,
sharpened switchbacks marked by
cliffhangs or banked by
deep ditches and thorny scrub,
narrowing paths and harrowing crawls.

The traveler am I,
moving forward,
always forward,
sometimes left, east,
northwest,
sometimes stopping, considering,
but never backwards,
unless only to go ahead again.
don't look back,
never look back,
but to see where you've been.
There's nothing behind you, except
what has been
and what is getting lost
in what is gone.

I am getting lost
in mucky struggle,
finding, floundering, failing,
flailing, but fighting always forward,
persevering, resisting,
pursuing progress no matter what,
endurance,
building strength, losing strength,
maybe not living,
but surviving.
Surviving is enough for now.
Finding forward,
endeavoring is enough
for now.

Serpentine/Schizophrenic

She lives in a body
too thin for her
with a man who builds
aquariums for her.
The words she says, she ties
to people's wrists
like helium balloons.
The words she writes
are hammers denting steel.
She can be described
in small words
with bigger meanings
or mysterious words
with secret meanings.
If wishes were birds,
she's waiting
for their wings to unlock.
She's waiting to unlock her.

Lines I wrote while falling asleep sleeping

fingers are freezing
windows are soggy and weeping
stones don't cause problems by themselves
emptiness fills the corners
plug bug
it's time to stop learning
the aspects of our uniforms are changing
winter is calling
the notebook is coming apart
in clumps I can be
we shiver in our lonely twitching sleep
colors slide from really dark to really light
be the place
claim to stay
thrive to try
don't go stray
can't strum a star
lean on nothing
use primer everywhere
decide to fall
from a poem to survival
we are locking ourselves in place
return to the wheel

A Pretty, Little Poem about some Fucked up Shit/The Horribly Horrible/The Unknown/Return to the Wheel

Too many words,
too few poems…
I'm composing mixed mashed lines
in my sleep. I dreamed
the skeleton inside me
is a slowly dismembering tumble
of knobbed and gnarled bones;
iron ribs filled with decaying bouquets;
and a tilted, painted skull,
perched precariously
on stone chipped vertebrae.

I'm eating my teeth.
If it can be broken
or hurt in my body,
then it already is.
Ensorcelled automagical electricity
is everywhere, except
within the leaky boundaries
of my attenuated heart,
which drips neither red nor blue.
Hardly thrumming,
languid, majestic and raw,
only lonely beats here.

Yearning for darkness,
the clouded circus sky

is a habituated pleasantry.
I keep trying to return to the wheel
like I told myself to do
in dream sleep. I don't know
what that means,
but I am trying to steer
away from the chasm
of the unknown, knowing that
there are no answers
in the deep valley.

The path out of Hell
is through misery
and finding beauty
in sadness.
Even when suffering is removed,
there is still pain.
For the emotionally amputated like me,
we cannot unstubborn ourselves
by being stubborn
and willfull.
So we should not,
can not
give up without trying.

Because occasionally,
even seldomly
the world is too gorgeous.
With all the lies I've been hiding,
I wasn't thinking,

wasn't feeling
when I said goodbye,
I don't care.
There is something wrong with me,
something overlooked,
bewildered,
something more
that I keep expecting to have to accept.

Something dissociated,
revocated,
something that requires loving,
tempering,
something huge,
inhuman and bestial,
something which I don't know
what it is.
It is something
unseen and held
at the bottom of myself,
something so alone
and so scared
and so born out of chaos.

January, June, August, October,
let me go.
Let me Fall,
Spring, Summer,
this Winter Child.
Give me up.

Give up in me.
Return me to the wheel.
I'm all crazy here.

It wasn't when
I raided my past,
but when I tried to walk
on water
that I started to drown.
And so now,
I will return
to the wheel,
over and again.
I will return
to the wheel.

Disappropriation

I knew I'd marry you
before I fell in love with you,
then I desperately loved
the slender curve of your collarbone.
I just never knew how to love you,
how to be more vulnerable, less vulnerable,
how to be vulnerable and not ashamed,
ashamed and not hurt,
hurt and not raw,
raw and not afraid,
not afraid absolutely.

I didn't know, don't know
how to love me, love you, love us,
love anyone or anything anyhow.
So I'd like to give up now please,
give up on everything except you.
The vast depth of your efforts,
your supports, your tries and carings,
the planets in your eyes,
the sweep of your bones
are all that are left of me,
all that keep me.

Life amidst Dying

It will be my curse to die of old age,
speaking the rusty, ancient,
chilling language of chains;
the vocabulary of the ending world.

I've been unhappy my entire life
and so assume
I'll be thus until the rest
as well also too.
Living is what happens
between deaths,
making man a fleeting shadow
that thrives in the rain
and dissolves when the sun breaks clouds.

Deprimental

Push against the sky.
Puff out clouds.
Bury the ground.
Raise a tree.
Float a bird before the green.

I'm starting to notice
When I'm not noticing
the thoughts I'm thinking.
There are so many ways
to be mindless.

It's so simple to not value anything.
When you value nothing.
Anger is a smoke screen.
Hope is a skill.
Love is a triumph.

It's so much easier
to have compassion for others,
because I actually
like other people,
occasionally.

Chaos is being stuck in emotions,
allowing them to fester,
multiple, evolve
until you become

vulnerable to yourself.

We need our emotions,
for their messages,
unless they are actively
destroying us,
unmeshing us.

Illness is when normalcy
overly impacts us detrimentally
causing us to want to quit,
decomposing us
and still we endure.
Somehow.

Contemplation #7

Through wavy windows I watch
my secret tree bend,
bounce,
sway and throw
in the wily wind
that Autumn has turned the other way.

Beneath vibrant orange
and dulling red,
highlit yellow and neon apple green
is stowed away
and only seen
illuminating the core from underneath.

Behind, it
is unknown whether
darkening grey or tawny white
is the sky
or clumsily careening clouds.

In contemplating the branches,
I realize they are like roots
veining strongly upwards.
I have been considering myself
the dashing colors
bounding in the breeze
and not as the stability
digging deeply into the earth unseen.

Splash

I need to do something
I can't do anything
mostly I'm in
occasionally I'm not
Akathesia

I am not my emotions
feelings are slaughtering me
perhaps it's time
that murders me
Exquisite Corpse

loneliness inhibits me
from embracing confusion
from being more than vacant
from testing possibilities
Hypotenuse

I'm contemplating the gravity of scars
assessing my attraction to an asteroid
cosigning my contract with a comet
guessing at the composition of stars
Orion

it's difficult to change
the shape of a convinced mind
to free a convicted heart
I'm constantly hiding in colors
Chameleon

My Icarus Ideations

Falling is all I believe in anymore.
it has been so long
since I've seen lightning
that I have forgotten
what it is for.
There are stars caught
in the barren branches and black
sky without edges.
Days are most delicate
just before dawn,
when all is so quiet
and nothing is still,
perfect for a creature such as me:
a monster molded out of pavement,
broken glass, gasoline
unlit matches
and a heart made of mud.
I'm not just dangerous,
I'm in danger.
My fingers are fit only for fighting.

I'll give you everything
you already know:
the wind and trees.
I'll teach you the language of bones:
all curves, precarious connections
and white, fragile fear.
We can whisper to each other
about freckles and fossas.
My hands are more honest
than my eyes,
more worthy than ribs.

There is you,
there is me
and the skeletons that hold us
together under the skull moon,
the soundlessness of spirit
and the draw.
It's where we break
that makes us beautiful.
We are what we do,
until we die.

I want to touch the world again,
love wonder,
love you like you need,
watch your brown eyes blue,
yellow and green
while they watch mine,
steel and pupil.
I want to climb
into your sad, sad song
that I've written for you
and wing us away
from the Icarus ideations
that hide in me.

It's my personal civil war
that is defeating us.

My Icarus Ideations Reversed

Defeating us,
is my personal civil war
that hides in me
from my Icarus Ideations.
Wing us away,
that which I've written for you.
Into your sad, sad song,
I want to climb,
all steel and pupil.

While they watch mine,
yellow and green,
I watch your brown eyes blue.
to love you like you need;
to love wonder
with the rain again;
to be in love,
I want to touch the world again.

Until we die,
we are what we do,
that makes us beautiful.
It's where we break,
the draw,
the soundlessness of spirit,
being together
under the skull moon
and the skeletons that hold us.
There is you
and there is me.
More worthy than ribs,
than eyes,
my hands are more honest

about freckles and fossas.
We can whisper to each other
with white, fragile fear.
All curves, precarious connections:
I'll teach you the language of bones,
the wind and trees.
You already know,
I'll give you everything.

My fingers are fit
only for fighting.
I'm in danger,
I'm not just dangerous.
A heart made of mud,
unlit matches,
broken glass and gasoline:
a monster molded out of pavement.
Perfect for a creature such as me,
when nothing is still
when all is so quiet,
just before dawn
is when days are most delicate.
In the sky without edges,
in the barren branches and black,
there are stars caught.
What it's for,
that I have forgotten,
since I've seen lightning.
Falling is all I believe in anymore.

Wraith:

A ghost or ghostlike image
of someone,
especially one seen shortly before
or after their death;
a pale, thin or insubstantial thing;
a wisp
or faint trace of something;
me;
an apparition;
tendrils of haze
over powdery snow;
fading fog;
transparent smoke
raising from smoldering ashes;
a malcontent;
a misfit;
a misanthrope;
a valueless death eater;
the tenuousness of a shattered soul;
the vacuity left
by a staggering silhouette;
a haggard;
the ambiviousness of bone deep,
hallucinatory,
recalcitrant, roiling,
wonderful and terrible –
the Riddle of Existence;
the punished;

a purloined spirit made of fist;
the bearded face of madness;
heaven and hell
as they both exist
as parts of this poor Earth;
an angel; a devil;
nothing;
absolutely, irrevocably nothing.

Dream/(After Tumult)

She floats above
the crow
of her own oxygen
and swoops down to kiss.

I still see her in my dreams,
wearing the sky loosely.

My friend,
my partner,
my lover,
my wife,
my no one.

The whole wide world
is moving
and there is iron
in my heart.
My belly full of fear.

I'm drowning all the time
in spiders and tears.
Shinning eyes
no longer set me free.

Weary

I'm getting lost in time,
lost in myself.
Time is getting lost in me.
I can't figure out what
the clouds are doing
to the sun and the stars.
I am nothing to the sky
and no one to the measuring.
My halves whisper to each other
in struggling silence.
They talk of horror and beauty,
regret and sadness,
anger and strength,
lust and decline.

I'm getting lost in time,
lost in myself.
Time is getting lost in me.
The dead hours of the day
happen somewhere between dusk
and dawn and still
no one has ever drowned
in the darkness.
Eventually all is yielded to
the growing of the light.

Time is getting lost in me.
Not just the moment wants me

expired.
I've never wanted more
so little a thing.
Yesterday is gone,
today is done
and tomorrow is not.
I turn to midnight,
sliding into the shadowed corner.

I'm getting lost in time.
The world beside me dreams
a gloomy morning,
wrapped in fists of bone.
The curled fingers
hold white mysteries.
I'm a ghost restrained
by skin and sinew.
I'll be anything except weak,
but I just keep breaking into eyes.

I'm getting lost in myself,
chronicling my own life.
My gift of doom
is that I forget
what I am built of.
Men of metal and screws
need to constantly adjust
their fit.
My name is night,
that is what the skull sky told me.

Time is getting lost.
Some days are a raven
silhouetted in a windy doorway,
contorted by lightning and thunder
in a mythical, mathematical storm
and distorted thoughts
that stalk the rain
and diverge trees
from their branches.
The bird becomes invisible.

I'm getting lost in me,
lost in myself.
Everything is always falling
all the time,
dragging me from my will.
Put me in a world where I can tell
smoke from fog,
sand from ash,
pain from hurt,
contentment from pride,
being lost from freedom,
tools from weapons
and nothing
from brokenness.

So Long

Here it comes again —
that fulminating feeling,
building,
the need,
that want to give up.
Quit;
the growing concern of danger
that I am to myself,
of what I can do
if I finally decide.
These emotions happen
faster than the speed of thought.

The world isn't a mystery.
It's a quick fall death trap
that no one survives.
Hope is a lie.
Suffering never ends.
All I ever wanted
is to be simple,
kind, uncomplicated.
All the things I turned out not to be.
Seeing outside this dungeon
of myself
only makes me sad.

I am no weapon of wisdom.
I have no existential intelligence.

I'm just a man
made of failure
and regret,
endowed with the lingering,
lawlessness of a suicidal pathway
and no virtue.
What is left of me
is pain
and loneliness.
They have been so much
a part of me
for so long,
I don't know if I would exist
without them.

I'm tired.
I'm weary.
I'm worn out.
Whatever I become
has to be different
than what I was
before.
Despair.

Convergence

I was holding you again.
We were kissing
so soft
and so sweet
when I woke up
in a mental institution.
Remembered.
(suddenly sad and defeated)

I am a statue:
stoic,
still,
sitting on the edge of the bed,
staring at the wall.
Purposeless.
Pent up.
Dire.
Dread.

wither

the trees resist
the bare wind
wanting for rain

confusing the clouds
with the destruction
of the Fall

the wasting away
withering leaves
the effort of leaving

the desperate twist
of empty branches
mossy torture

red orange yellow green
dry brown grass
white sky

always a student
of perpetual seasons
sorting out solitude from silence

death is pretty
like too much wine
and seamless dreams

Owl Us Universe

There's an owl outside the window,
talking to the wind.
The night is a train
in the snowy distance.

It's black outside my heart.
I have no home.
I don't think
I understand
what that means
to a soul without wings.

Some freedom
is too much freedom.
I'd rather be closed
in a keyless cage
or buried beneath the sound
of the universe doing.

Midnight

It's difficult to tell
the fog from the grass,
the air from the sky,
the cold from the night.
It's hard to tell my body not to feel.

I can't stop the pain.
I can't stop the light
from glowing.
The movement continues.
The trees tower.

I tried to give you my love.
Failed.
I could live inside your rain,
so soft and so deep,
so full of longing.

Flickering.
Flutter.
Flow.
The moon is a star
pulling at me.

Anyway/Anhedonia

There's pain in everything,
sadness,
cold in the morning bones,
every day is a skirmish.
Tired fingers and cramped hands
give up the war,
lay down their arms.

All through the long darkness
have I striven;
frozen moon,
muddy regret.
Peering behind the wind,
there's nothing moving it,
just will
and scared horse's eyes.

It's strange and wild
in a failed dream.
I guess I'll go back
to being invisible.
I'm better
when I don't matter.
I'm just mist anyway.

I'm grieving
the losses of my life,
the time I've whiled away,

the wishes and wantings
I've given up
in pursuit of living,
surviving, trying
to stay alive.
I can't get myself to do anything anymore.
I'm just bits of star dust anyway,
cocooned in this pitiful body.

Teach us salvation in this grief.
Show us mercy in our decline.
Give us this day our daily night.
Tempt us not with our catastrophes.
Corral us against our game with death,
our sour wanderings.
Forgive us our yearnings.
Forget us our penance.
Please us with our beauty.
Let us go
or make us dead.

Eulogy / A Funeral Address

Sailor.
Landlord.
Financier.
Workaholic.
Meticulous.
Perfectionist.
Re-arranger.
Organizer.
Inquisitor.
Hoarder of information.
Computer.
Engineer.
Fixer.
Tinkerer.
Rule breaker.
Joker.
Friend.

It's difficult to rename a person,
to make concise a life,
especially when people
are so hard to know.
Enigma.
Words fail feelings.
Memories fail words.

All the decades can't be
monkey-barred across
and still,
it's so easy to grieve
the loss
of a figure so permanent,
suddenly made so fleeting.

His love was always bread.

Not always there.
Always a presence.
Always stable,
predictable.
Always an uncertainty.
Always near and far,
both.

Interested in interests.
Every topic something to discuss,
an opening to wander through
in the large mind
of someone so tall
and so content to be
just a man.

Classical.
Educated.
Self-educated.
Motivated by modern.
Current.
Involved.
Unevolved.
Unrefined.
Undefinable.
Unfinished.
Gone.

Farewell father.
We love you.

Glimmer

I wasn't borne for all of this
blood, battle and iron,
but to sit quiet in a room,
with just my echo,
my shadow and me.

I was made for the darkness,
a rusty wolf in the rain.
Everything has lost its shine;
I'm only happy when I'm dreaming.
I miss having skin.

Because there is no way back,
all I want is to sleep.
I'm screaming on the inside.
I don't feel love,
only loss and longing.

I miss my life.

About Atmosphere Press

Atmosphere Press is an independent, full-service publisher for excellent books in all genres and for all audiences. Learn more about what we do at atmospherepress.com.

We encourage you to check out some of Atmosphere's latest releases, which are available at Amazon.com and via order from your local bookstore:

A Synonym for Home, poetry by Kimberly Jarchow
The Cry of Being Born, poetry by Carol Mariano
Big Man Small Europe, poetry by Tristan Niskanen
In the Cloakroom of Proper Musings, a lyric narrative by Kristina Moriconi
Lucid_Malware.zip, poetry by Dylan Sonderman
The Unordering of Days, poetry by Jessica Palmer
It's Not About You, poetry by Daniel Casey
A Dream of Wide Water, poetry by Sharon Whitehill
Radical Dances of the Ferocious Kind, poetry by Tina Tru
The Woods Hold Us, poetry by Makani Speier-Brito
My Cemetery Friends: A Garden of Encounters at Mount Saint Mary in Queens, New York, nonfiction and poetry by Vincent J. Tomeo
Report from the Sea of Moisture, poetry by Stuart Jay Silverman
The Enemy of Everything, poetry by Michael Jones
The Stargazers, poetry by James McKee
The Pretend Life, poetry by Michelle Brooks
Minnesota and Other Poems, poetry by Daniel N. Nelson

About the Author

Daniel J. Lutz graduated from the University of Iowa with a degree in English and received a Master's in Nursing from the University of DePaul. He currently works as a Hospice Nurse and lives in Libertyville, IL.

This is the second volume of poetry published by the author. The first being: *Thoughts, Perceptions and Other Miscellaneous Abstractions*, published in 1998.

CPSIA information can be obtained
at www.ICGtesting.com
Printed in the USA
LVHW110731030321
680446LV00006B/373